Extreme Sports

SKYDIVING

DiscoverRoo
An Imprint of Pop!
popbooksonline.com

Matt Scheff

abdobooks.com

Published by Pop!, a division of ABDO, PO Box 398166, Minneapolis, Minnesota 55439.

Printed in the United States of America, North Mankato, Minnesota.

052020
092020

THIS BOOK CONTAINS RECYCLED MATERIALS

Cover Photo: Shutterstock Images
Interior Photos: Shutterstock Images, 1, 8–9, 12, 13, 17, 21, 27, 28, 29, 31; iStockphoto, 5, 6, 7, 11, 14, 15, 18, 19, 20, 22–23, 30; Shekhar Yadav/The India Today Group/Getty Images, 25

Editor: Brienna Rossiter
Series Designer: Jake Slavik

Library of Congress Control Number: 2019954957

Publisher's Cataloging-in-Publication Data

Names: Scheff, Matt, author.

Title: Skydiving / by Matt Scheff

Description: Minneapolis, Minnesota : POP!, 2021 | Series: Extreme sports | Includes online resources and index.

Identifiers: ISBN 9781532167867 (lib. bdg.) | ISBN 9781532168963 (ebook)

Subjects: LCSH: Skydiving--Juvenile literature. | Parachutists--Juvenile literature. | Sky divers--Juvenile literature. | Extreme sports--Juvenile literature. | Sports--Juvenile literature.

Classification: DDC 796.046--dc23

Pop open this book and you'll find QR codes loaded with information, so you can learn even more!

Scan this code* and others like it while you read, or visit the website below to make this book pop!

popbooksonline.com/skydiving

*Scanning QR codes requires a web-enabled smart device with a QR code reader app and a camera.

TABLE OF CONTENTS

CHAPTER 1

TIME TO JUMP

An airplane soars 13,000 feet (4,000 m) above the ground. The plane's side door opens. Wind rushes in. Two skydivers stand ready. It's time for them to jump. They leap from the plane's door.

WATCH A VIDEO HERE!

Skydivers often jump from heights of 10,000 to 18,000 feet (3,000–5,500 m).

Skydivers who jump from greater heights have more time in free fall.

The skydivers zoom through the air. For almost 60 seconds, they are in **free fall**. As the ground rushes closer, the skydivers release their **parachutes**.

Bright fabric stretches out above them.

It catches the air and slows their fall.

Steering lines attach to the parachute's sides. Skydivers pull on them to steer.

The skydivers drift slowly to the ground. Then they land on their feet. Their parachutes flop down behind them. The skydivers pack up their gear. They check it for safety. Soon they'll be ready to do it all over again.

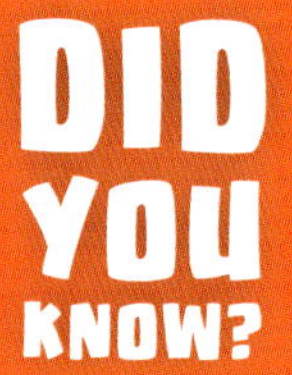

After opening their parachutes, most skydivers drift for five to seven minutes.

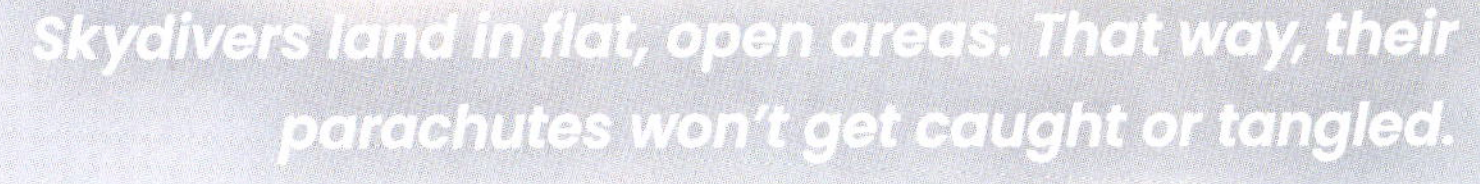

Skydivers land in flat, open areas. That way, their parachutes won't get caught or tangled.

CHAPTER 2

HISTORY OF SKYDIVING

People have been skydiving for more than 200 years. In 1797, André-Jacques Garnerin made the world's first skydiving jump. He used a hot-air balloon and a silk **parachute**. Garnerin had a hard

LEARN MORE HERE!

André-Jacques Garnerin rode a hot-air balloon over Paris, France, to make the first skydiving jump.

landing. But his parachute worked. He had invented a thrilling new sport.

Early parachutes were attached to hot-air balloon baskets. The parachutes pulled away when people jumped.

Early parachutes didn't always work well. Some jumpers were hurt or killed.

Over time, people found better designs and stronger materials. In the 1900s, airplanes were invented. Parachutes became important safety devices. They helped people escape the airplanes if something went wrong.

Later parachutes attached to a harness worn on the person's body.

In tandem skydiving, two divers jump together and share a parachute.

As parachutes improved, skydiving grew as a thrill sport. Some skydivers jumped together in large groups. Others broke records for speed and height.

A wingsuit has flaps of fabric between the legs and between the arms and body.

SKYDIVING RECORDS

Skydivers have made some amazing jumps. In 2016, Henrik Raimer set a speed record. He fell at 373.6 miles per hour (601.3 km/h). In 2014, Alan Eustace set a record for the highest jump ever. He fell from more than 25 miles (40 km) off the ground. That's near the edge of outer space! And in 2016, Kyle Lobpries used a wingsuit to glide for 19.94 miles (32.1 km).

DID YOU KNOW?

A wingsuit increases a skydiver's surface area. Fabric flaps catch the air and allow the skydiver to glide.

CHAPTER 3

SKYDIVING TODAY

Today, skydivers use state-of-the-art gear. The most important piece of gear is the **parachute**. Modern parachutes are made of strong, light fabric. Nylon is the most common fabric.

COMPLETE AN ACTIVITY HERE!

Parachutes come in a variety of shapes. Many are round or rectangular.

Most skydivers wear parachutes in packs on their backs. The main chute is called the **canopy**. Divers also use a **pilot chute**. They pull a cord to release the pilot chute first. A line connects it to the canopy. The pilot chute pulls the canopy out of the pack. Then, the canopy can open up. It creates **air resistance**. This force slows a skydiver's fall.

FORCES IN SKYDIVING

1. When the skydiver jumps from the plane, air resistance is less than the skydiver's weight. The speed of the skydiver's fall increases.

2. As speed increases, so does air resistance. Eventually, weight and air resistance balance, and the skydiver falls at a steady speed.

3. When the parachute opens, air resistance becomes greater than the skydiver's weight. The skydiver's speed slows.

In formation skydiving, many divers jump at once. They link arms and legs to form shapes.

Some skydivers jump just for fun. Others compete. Formation skydiving is one of the most popular events. In this style of skydiving, teams jump as groups.

A freestyle skydiver strikes a pose.

They work together to form patterns. Divers hold on to one another as they move through the air.

Freestyle skydiving is also common. These divers do tricks to impress judges. They spin, twist, and flip as they fall.

A skydiver aims to land on a small disk.

Accuracy landing is all about steering. Jumpers try to land as close as possible to a disk on the ground. The disk is just 1.9 inches (5 cm) wide. High-tech sensors record where each jumper lands. The jumper who gets closest wins.

DID YOU KNOW?

In 2006, a group called World Team set a record for the biggest formation. It included 400 skydivers!

SUPERSTAR

SHITAL MAHAJAN-RANE

- Shital Mahajan-Rane of India has made more than 700 skydiving jumps.

- She has set several skydiving world records.

- Mahajan-Rane has jumped over both the North and South Poles. The jump over the North Pole took place in 2004. It was her first time skydiving! The South Pole jump took place in 2006.

- In 2017, she became the first woman to skydive over all seven continents.

Shital Mahajan-Rane (right) received an award from India's president in 2011.

- Her highest skydive was from a height of 30,500 feet (9,300 m).
- She set one record while wearing a wingsuit. Wingsuits can be very hard to control. Skydivers need special skills and training to use them.

CHAPTER 4

SAFETY

Skydiving involves great speed and heights. As a result, it can be very risky. Skydivers train in the proper ways to jump, fall, and land. They learn how to react if they experience problems with their gear.

LEARN MORE HERE!

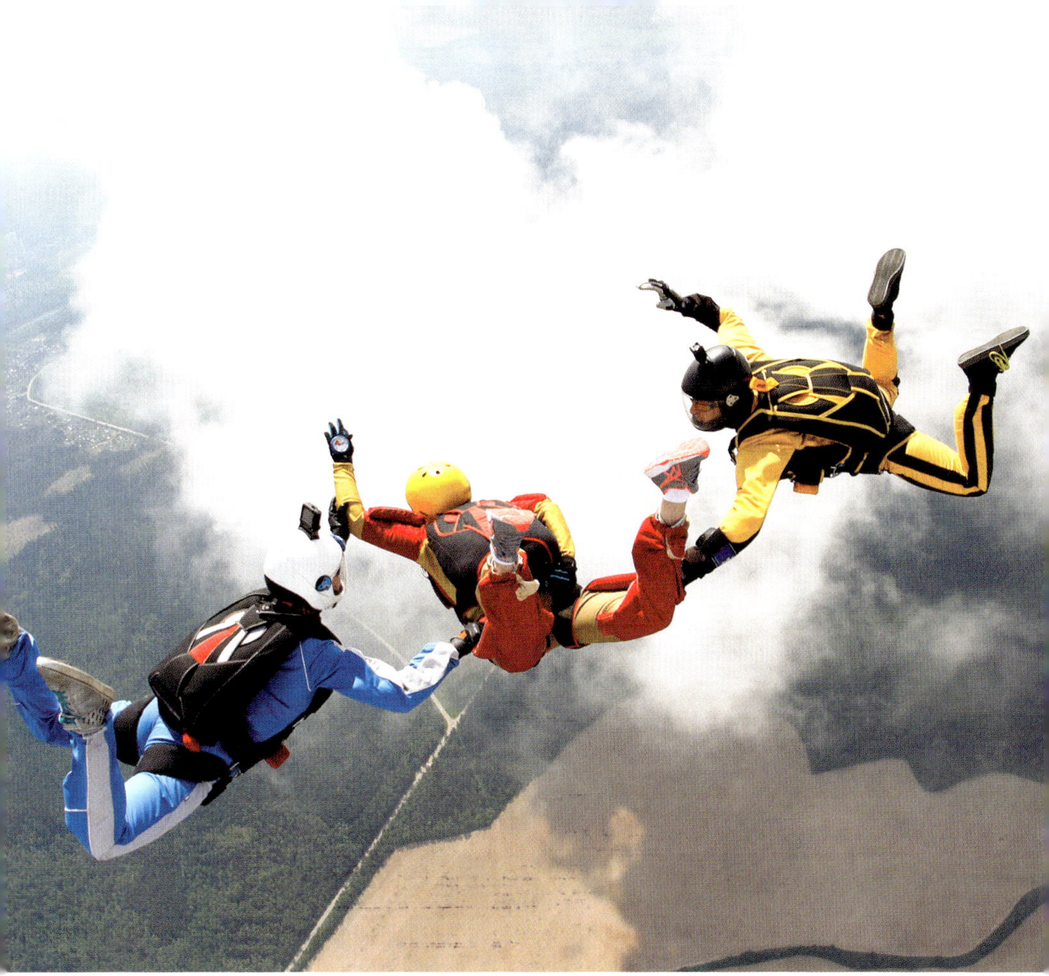

Two instructors help a student learn how to open a parachute.

DID YOU KNOW?

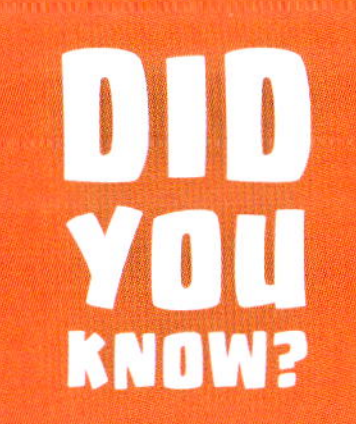

Skydivers fall at speeds of more than 120 miles per hour (190 km/h).

A system of three rings on the harness can quickly release the main parachute if it fails.

Each diver carries a reserve chute. A diver uses it if the **canopy** doesn't work. Many divers also use a device that automatically releases the reserve chute if something goes wrong.

Skydivers **inspect** their gear before each jump. With proper gear and care, skydiving can be a fun and thrilling sport.

A skydiver packs a parachute to prepare for a jump.

MAKING CONNECTIONS

TEXT-TO-SELF

Would you ever want to try skydiving? Why or why not?

TEXT-TO-TEXT

Have you read books about other sports that require safety gear? What sports are they, and what gear do they use?

TEXT-TO-WORLD

How has skydiving changed over the years? How might it change in the future?

GLOSSARY

accuracy – being able to hit an intended target.

air resistance – the force of air that pushes back against a moving object.

canopy – the large fabric part of a parachute.

free fall – falling rapidly toward the ground as a result of gravity.

inspect – to look over something carefully.

parachute – a device used to slow the speed of a falling person or object.

pilot chute – a small parachute that a skydiver releases to open the main canopy.

INDEX

ONLINE RESOURCES

popbooksonline.com

Scan this code* and others like it while you read, or visit the website below to make this book pop!

popbooksonline.com/skydiving

*Scanning QR codes requires a web-enabled smart device with a QR code reader app and a camera.